T0303422

RAND

RYAN ANDREW BROWN, TODD C. HELMUS,
RAJEEV RAMCHAND

Veteran Narratives of Support for Extremist Groups and Beliefs

Results from Interviews with Members of a Nationally Representative Survey of the U.S. Veteran Community

For more information on this publication, visit **www.rand.org/t/RRA1071-4**.

Published by the RAND Corporation, Santa Monica, Calif.

Library of Congress Cataloging-in-Publication Data is available for this publication.

ISBN: 978-1-9774-1310-9

Cover photo: Chad Davis from United States, CC BY 2.0, via Wikimedia Commons

About This Report

This report details findings from interviews with select members of a nationally representative survey of U.S. military veterans regarding their support for specific extremist groups—Antifa, Proud Boys, Black nationalists, and White supremacists—as well as their endorsement of beliefs associated with such groups, including support for political violence, belief in the QAnon conspiracy, and belief in the Great Replacement theory. The report examines how veterans describe their extremist beliefs, their experiences in the military and in transition to veteran status, and their narratives of the path to their current beliefs.

This project was conducted through a collaboration with the RAND Epstein Family Veterans Policy Research Institute and the Justice Policy Program within RAND Social and Economic Well-Being.

RAND Epstein Family Veterans Policy Research Institute

The RAND Epstein Family Veterans Policy Research Institute is dedicated to conducting innovative, evidence-based research and analysis to improve the lives of those who have served in the U.S. military. Building on decades of interdisciplinary expertise at the RAND Corporation, the institute prioritizes creative, equitable, and inclusive solutions and interventions that meet the needs of diverse veteran populations while engaging and empowering those who support them. For more information about the RAND Epstein Family Veterans Policy Research Institute, visit www.veterans.rand.org. Questions about this report or about the RAND Epstein Family Veterans Policy Research Institute should be directed to veteranspolicy@rand.org.

Justice Policy Program

RAND Social and Economic Well-Being is a division of RAND that seeks to actively improve the health and social and economic well-being of populations and communities throughout the world. This research was conducted in the Justice Policy Program within RAND Social and Economic Well-Being. The program focuses on such topics as access to justice, policing, corrections, drug policy, and court system reform, as well as other policy concerns pertaining to public safety and criminal and civil justice. For more information, email justicepolicy@rand.org.

Funding

Funding for this publication was made possible by a generous gift from Daniel J. Epstein through the Epstein Family Foundation, which established the RAND Epstein Family Veterans Policy Research Institute in 2021, and the Pritzker Military Foundation, on behalf of the Pritzker Military Museum & Library.

Acknowledgments

We are grateful to the Pritzker Military Foundation on behalf of the Pritzker Military Museum & Library and the RAND Epstein Family Veterans Policy Institute for their generous financial support of this project. We would also like to thank our reviewers, Colin P. Clarke of the Soufan Center and Caitlin McCulloch of RAND for their helpful critiques and guidance. We are eternally grateful to the veterans who have made so many sacrifices for our national security, including those veterans who are part of the National Opinion Research Center's AmeriSpeak® Panel and who completed the interviews for this study.

Summary

Throughout 2023, we conducted 21 interviews with military veterans from a 2022 representative survey of nearly 1,000 veterans in the United States who had indicated support for one or more extremist groups or beliefs to understand the drivers and patterns of extremism among veterans. This is the first study to use interview data to understand how veteran experiences may be linked to support for extremist groups and radical ideologies.

Participants offered a heterogeneous set of responses when asked whether they currently supported extremist groups or causes during the survey in 2022. Almost all interview participants who had supported the Proud Boys in the 2022 survey denied such support during interviews, while nearly all the participants who affirmed support for the Great Replacement on the 2022 survey believed that the Democratic Party was attempting to purchase votes through lax immigration policies. Many participants affirmed support for the potential necessity of political violence, although the responses suggested that none of the interviewees were intent on acting on such support.

Roughly three-quarters (15 of 21) of our interviewees reported a negative or traumatic life event while in the military, ranging from interpersonal conflict (often leading to discharge) to combat trauma to physical and sexual abuse. Twelve respondents described having difficulties with the transition from military to civilian life, including missing the pace and camaraderie of military life, having no resources; not knowing where to turn for help or support; struggling with posttraumatic stress disorder or depression; experiencing homelessness; and becoming imprisoned.

Twelve of our 21 respondents provided narratives of life experiences that helped push them toward more-extreme political viewpoints, including specific events in the United States or international politics and history, experiences during deployment or work settings, and life disruptions during the coronavirus disease 2019 pandemic. Twelve of our interviewees explained how they were socialized into radical viewpoints through friends or family and/or how their social circles provide support and encouragement for radical beliefs and support of radical groups.

Seventeen respondents mentioned specific media sources, social media platforms, and podcasters or political influencers that helped shape their viewpoints, ranging from CNN and Fox News to Russia Today and Newsmax, from Facebook to specific Reddit or Telegram channels, and from podcaster Joe Rogan to television host George Stephanopoulos.

Because of the small sample size and no interviews with those who did not endorse extremist groups or beliefs, it is impossible to draw causal connections between military or transition experiences and support for extremist groups or beliefs in this study. Future work should leverage surveys and interviews with a larger sample of individuals to determine causal pathways between military and veteran life experiences and outcomes related to extremism.

Contents

Tables

CHAPTER 1

Introduction

The January 6, 2021, events on Capitol Hill and subsequent prosecutions, as well as recent analysis, have raised concerns about people with military experience joining extremist causes and conducting violent attacks. Scholars, for example, have estimated that approximately 13.5 percent to 17 percent of those prosecuted for the Capitol Hill attacks on January 6 were either currently or in the past affiliated with the U.S. military,[1] although veterans constitute only 6.2 percent of the U.S. adult population.[2] Furthermore, veterans have made up four of the five members of Proud Boys leadership indicted by federal prosecutors on seditious conspiracy.[3] In addition, research by the National Consortium for the Study of Terrorism and Responses to Terrorism (START) suggests that individuals with veteran status are increasingly being documented among those known to have committed criminal acts driven by political, economic, social, or religious motivations.[4] Finally, START most recently found that (1) having a military background was the single strongest predictor of involvement in a mass casualty attack in the United States from 1990 to 2021 and (2) having a military background increased the lethality of attacks by up to two times.[5]

Prompted, in part, by these trends, RAND researchers conducted a nationally representative survey of U.S. veterans in 2022. This survey research indicated that veterans appeared to

---

1 George Washington University Program on Extremism, "Capitol Hill Siege: Demographics Tracker"; Jensen, Kane, and Akers, "Extremism in the Ranks and After"; U.S. Census Bureau, "Veterans Day 2023: November 11." One potential difference between these two datasets is that the START program includes four individuals facing charges for refusing to leave U.S. Capitol grounds after a curfew was imposed on the evening of January 6, 2021, and the one Air Force veteran who was killed while breaching the capitol.

2 Subsequent analysis has determined that, given the age and other characteristics of January 6 participants, veterans were not statistically more likely to be involved than other individuals. See Levine et al., *Prohibited Extremist Activities in the U.S. Department of Defense.*

3 Toropin and Beynon, "Veterans Make Up Most of Proud Boys Members Indicted on Sedition for Jan 6 Violence."

4 Jensen, Kane, and Akers, "Extremism in the Ranks and After."

5 Jensen, Kane, and Akers, *Mass Casualty Extremist Offenders with U.S. Military Backgrounds.*

support such extremist groups as Antifa,[6] Proud Boys,[7] and White supremacist groups at a rate lower than the general population and appeared to believe in QAnon,[8] the Great Replacement theory, and the use of political violence at levels close to the general U.S. population (see Table 1.1 for survey items representing these beliefs).[9]

However, as subsequent studies and reports have pointed out, veteran involvement in extremism may constitute a "small numbers, high impact" problem.[10] This factor further raises the stakes of understanding the pathways through which veterans may come to hold extremist beliefs or become involved in extremist groups and causes. However, no qualitative study has yet been published that elucidates when, where, why, and how veterans may become involved with extremist causes and extremist groups.

In this study, we recruited individuals who participated in the 2022 RAND survey and who had affirmed support for extremist groups or causes to engage in qualitative interviews. During these interviews, we asked veterans to describe their support for extremist groups or causes and detail their military experiences, civilian experiences, and political beliefs. We were able to interview 21 veterans on this topic (six with left-leaning ideologies and 15 with right-leaning ideologies), with several interviews lasting one hour or more.

This report details our findings from these interviews, which revealed the considerable presence of negative and traumatic life events for interviewees while in the military and afterward while trying to adapt to civilian life. Coupled with narratives of becoming involved in extremist ideas and groups, these narratives point to several possible implications for policy and practice, which in turn will require further research to design, test, and calibrate.

---

6 For a description of Antifa and related groups, see Jones, Doxsee, and Harrington, *The Escalating Terrorism Problem in the United States.*

7 The Proud Boys are a right-wing group that first hit news headlines during the Unite the Right rally in Virginia in 2017 and were involved in the January 6, 2021, riot at the U.S. Capitol. For more details, see Kutner, "Swiping Right"; and Rothbart and Stebbins, "The Proud Boys Raging Righteously at the US Capitol on January 6, 2021."

8 QAnon is described as follows: "Decentralized, far-right political movement rooted in a baseless conspiracy theory that the world is controlled by the 'Deep state,' a cabal of Satan-worshipping pedophiles, and that former President Donald Trump is the only person who can defeat it" (see Anti-Defamation League, "QAnon").

9 Helmus, Brown, and Ramchand, *Prevalence of Veteran Support for Extremist Groups and Extremist Beliefs.*

10 For example, see Jensen, Yates, and Kane, *Radicalization in the Ranks*; Anne Speckhard, and Molly Ellenberg, *An Analysis of Active-Duty and Veteran Military Members Involved in White Supremacist and Violent Anti-Government Militias and Groups*; and recent congressional testimony on the topic at Jones, "Violent Domestic Extremist Groups and the Recruitment of Veterans."

Methods and Sample

In our 2022 study, we conducted surveys with a nationally representative sample of approximately 1,000 U.S. veterans who are part of AmeriSpeak, a probability-based panel maintained and managed by the National Opinion Research Center (NORC). As part of that survey study, we asked respondents whether they supported one or more extremist groups or extremist beliefs (see Table 1.1).[11] More information on the sample is presented in our previous publication.[12]

TABLE 1.1
Support for Extremist Groups and Ideologies: Survey Questions

Support for (group or belief):	Question Text	Response Options
Antifa	What is your opinion of Antifa?	☐ Very favorable ☐ Somewhat favorable ☐ Heard of, no opinion ☐ Somewhat unfavorable ☐ Very unfavorable ☐ Never heard of
Proud Boys	What is your opinion of Proud Boys?	
Black nationalists	What is your opinion of Black Nationalists (Nation of Islam, Five Percent Nation, New Black Panthers, etc.)?	
White supremacists	What is your opinion of White supremacists (KKK, Patriot Front, Aryan Brotherhood, etc.)?	
Please rate the extent to which you agree or disagree with the following:		
Political violence	Because things have gotten so far off track, true American patriots may have to resort to violence in order to save our country.	☐ Completely agree ☐ Mostly agree ☐ Mostly disagree ☐ Completely disagree
QAnon	The government, media, and financial worlds in the U.S. are controlled by a group of Satan-worshipping pedophiles who run a global child sex-trafficking operation.	
Great Replacement theory	A group of people in this country are trying to replace native-born Americans with immigrants and people of color who share their political views.	

NOTE: KKK = Ku Klux Klan.

[11] The study of extremism, radicalization, and radical ideologies is different than which groups are officially designated as terrorist organizations by the federal government (which is a topic of considerable ongoing debate).

[12] Helmus, Brown, and Ramchand, *Prevalence of Veteran Support for Extremist Groups and Extremist Beliefs*.

For this current study, NORC invited back all of the participants who had previously expressed support for one or more extremist groups ("very favorable") or one or more extremist beliefs ("completely agree") (N = 137) and who agreed to be contacted for a follow-up interview (N = 84) to participate in a recorded interview on the Zoom.gov platform to talk about their political beliefs and their experiences in the military and during the transition to civilian life. NORC attempted to schedule interviews with all 84 individuals who indicated they were willing to participate. Thirty-two of the 84 individuals signed up and scheduled interview appointments.

We conducted interviews between June 2023 and August 2023. Our overall no-show rate was 44 percent. However, we were able to reschedule many of these original no-shows. In total, 21 of the 32 individuals who scheduled appointments one or more times eventually completed interviews. We allowed participants to no-show and reschedule three times before NORC stopped trying to schedule additional appointments. After the first several interviews, we also increased our financial incentive from $40 to $60, which decreased our no-show rate. Final interview sample demographics for those 21 individuals are provided in Table 1.2, along with demographics for the eligible population and those who agreed to be recontacted for interviews.

TABLE 1.2
Sample Demographics for Interviews

	Eligible Sample, *N* (%)	Eligible Sample that Agreed to Be Contacted, *N* (%)	Interview Sample, *N*
Gender			
Male	128 (93.4%)	78 (92.9%)	19
Female	9 (6.6%)	6 (7.1%)	2
Age			
18–34	9 (6.6%)	5 (6.0%)	2
35–54	31 (22.6%)	20 (23.8%)	7
55–64	28 (20.4%)	19 (22.6%)	7
65+	69 (50.4%)	40 (47.6%)	5
Race/ethnicity			
White, non-Hispanic	100 (73.0%)	65 (77.4%)	12
Black, non-Hispanic	20 (14.6%)	11 (13.1%)	4
Other, non-Hispanic	10 (7.3%)	3 (3.6%)	2
Hispanic	7 (5.1%)	5 (6.0%)	3

TABLE 1.2—Continued

	Eligible Sample, *N* (%)	Eligible Sample that Agreed to Be Contacted, *N* (%)	Interview Sample, *N*
Socioeconomic status			
Educational attainment			
Less than high school	1 (0.7%)	1 (1.2%)	0
High school graduate or equivalent	17 (12.4%)	8 (9.5%)	1
Vocational school, technical school, some college, or associate degree	75 (54.7%)	47 (56.0%)	10
Bachelor's degree	20 (14.6%)	13 (15.5%)	4
Post-graduate study/professional degree	24 (17.5%)	15 (17.9%)	6
Household income			
Less than $30,000	23 (16.8%)	16 (19.1%)	2
$30,000 to less than $60,000	41 (29.9%)	22 (26.2%)	5
$60,000 to less than $100,000	35 (25.6%)	17 (20.2%)	3
$100,000 or more	38 (27.7%)	29 (34.5%)	11
Unemployed	15 (11.0%)	8 (9.5%)	1
Military service			
Service branch (not mutually exclusive)			
Army	53 (38.7%)	32 (38.1%)	10
Navy	33 (24.1%)	17 (20.2%)	3
Air Force	36 (26.3%)	27 (32.1%)	7
Marine Corps	16 (11.7%)	8 (9.5%)	1
When served			
Pre-9/11	103 (75.2%)	66 (78.6%)	14
Post-9/11	34 (24.8%)	18 (21.4%)	7
Opinions of U.S. political parties (not mutually exclusive)			
Find Democrats favorable	32 (23.4%)	20 (23.8%)	6
Find Republicans favorable	75 (54.7%)	49 (58.3%)	12

SOURCE: Features information from NORC AmeriSpeak veteran panel surveys, June–August 2023.

NOTE: 9/11 = September 11, 2001, terrorist attacks.

The lead author (Brown) led 14 of the interviews, and the second author (Helmus) led the remaining seven interviews. Interviews began with a discussion of the respondents' experiences in the military, then proceeded to talk about the transition to civilian life, and finally discussed political beliefs. We chose to enquire about participants' political beliefs at the end of the interview to first establish rapport with the participants before addressing potentially sensitive political beliefs. The interview instrument is provided in Appendix A. Interviews lasted between 40 minutes and 75 minutes, depending on the level of rapport and other interview dynamics (e.g., real-time interruptions in the respondent's environment, interviewees' comfort discussing different topics). All research activities were approved by RAND's Human Subjects Protection Committee (RAND's Institutional Review Board).

In all cases, Brown and Helmus either attended each other's interviews and took live (near verbatim) notes, or (if not able to attend live) listened to the interview recordings at a later point and produced notes from the recording. This resulted in near-verbatim notes from each interview.[13]

We consulted with each other throughout the interview process to discuss emerging themes and produced an interview coding matrix in Microsoft Excel based on the most prevalent topics discussed. The main topics in this interview matrix were divided into three main segments, each with its own subtopics: patterns of extremist beliefs; difficult experiences in military service and the transition to civilian life; and the path to current beliefs.

In the following sections, we provide the results of our rapid qualitative analysis, breaking out our findings by further patterns under each subtopic and also providing exemplary quotations along with information on sex/gender of the respondent and whether they tended to lean more right-wing or left-wing in their beliefs.[14] In all, we had six left-wing participants (five men, one woman) and 15 right-wing participants (14 men, one woman).

---

[13] This publication quotes and includes references to profanities. We included the wording and tenor of our participants' language because it is integral to the research and our findings presented in this report.

[14] This could often be determined by the respondent's survey responses, which included support for Democrats or Republicans as well as Proud Boys, Antifa, Black nationalists, and White supremacists. If the pattern of survey responses was unclear or seemed to support both sides, we used interview content to "break the tie."

CHAPTER 2

Patterns of Extremist Beliefs and Behaviors

During our 2023 interviews, we asked respondents to respond to the specific survey items of support for extremist groups and causes to which they had agreed in the original 2022 survey. We then asked participants to provide an explanation of their responses. The purpose of this effort was to better understand the ideology that undergirded their original support and to use their responses as a means of further exploring their political viewpoints. One key observation from this exercise is that individuals have complex and diverse motivations and rationales for their support of extremist groups and beliefs that underly individual responses to survey items. We also observed that participants at times retracted their original extremist positions, although many directly and confidently reaffirmed their support.

Antifa

We interviewed three participants who had expressed support for Antifa in our survey. In one case, a participant ultimately stated that he was "neutral or I don't know," but ". . . if the name is an inclination, then that sounds great." Two others were more supportive. One caveated his response by saying he did not think it was a "real organization" but that he was "kind of positive." He did not agree with Antifa's violence but if "people are in public flying Nazi flags, Antifa is going to be there" and "shouting them down." Another also stated that it was more a movement than a "real organization" but that "as a military person, that is what we fought against, we fought against fascism." He continued, "We will not allow our country to become like Nazi Germany."

Proud Boys

All of the four participants who had affirmed support for the Proud Boys on our previous survey denied their support during our 2023 interviews. One such participant was a self-described liberal who reported that he was kicked off Facebook for hate speech, which he vaguely described as "memes about Donald Trump." This individual anchored his opinions about the Proud Boys from the perspective of the organization's right to exist. "No thoughts, they are human beings and they have done nothing to me; trying to take over the Capitol is crazy, but I say we are all human beings and we should be treated equally." Another veteran reported that, despite leaning toward right-wing ideologies, he was otherwise not very political, and he observed that the January 6 event at the Capitol was a "terrorist attack." This veteran stated that "I am against Proud Boys," but then noted that he respected them because "they don't hide [their beliefs]. As long as you are honest and up front I can deal with that." A third veteran also described himself as a right-leaning moderate and noted that he voted for President Barack Obama before casting a vote for President Donald Trump. As he observed, "I never followed them, never understood what their meaning was. . . . they never popped up on my radar so I don't know much about them, never looked into it." A fourth participant described himself as a "hardline conservative" and, in the interview, he affirmed his support for both political violence and QAnon. However, he denied support for the Proud Boys, noting that he "strongly disapproved." "I don't know anyone who is a member of the Proud Boys. . . . I am their ideal candidate, but besides standing around in masks and yelling [at] people, I don't know what they do."

Black Nationalists

We interviewed three participants who had previously expressed support for Black nationalist groups, such as the Nation of Islam, Five Percent Nation, and the New Black Panthers. All had self-professed liberal views on politics. One participant was the same person who stated that the Proud Boys had a right to exist. This individual extended this attitude on liberty to the Black nationalists as he also seemed to do for the KKK by stating, "They all deserve to be heard like the KKK deserved to be heard." Two others justified their positive view of Black nationalists by noting the positive impact they reportedly had on their communities. One stated that he supported the Black Panthers because they "provided food to their communities" and had a lot of "community programs." He also noted that they are "unfortunately misunderstood" and blamed the government for sowing misinformation about the group and "whitewashing history." The third participant focused on how the Nation of Islam helped improve the lives of some of its members. He spoke of associates he knew who spent time in prison for burglary and selling drugs, and "they didn't go back to any of those because Nation of Islam taught them better." He said several members had asked him to join, but he did not want to and refused to join.

White Supremacists

Two participants affirmed support for white supremacists in the original survey. Now, when asked, neither supported the groups' ideologies. One participant, the same individual who previously stated they supported the Proud Boys and Black nationalists because of their right to exist, said the same about White supremacists: "They are an organization like we are, and they deserve to be out there like we deserve to be out there." The other outright denied support. "I don't get into any of that stuff. If you're a racial man in today's world, you're an idiot. It's just that simple."

Political Violence

Overall, ten participants, all professed political conservatives, had previously offered support for political violence by answering that they completely or mostly agreed with the statement: "Because things have gotten so far off track, true American patriots may have to resort to violence in order to save our country." During the interview, these participants expressed varying levels of support for this item.

Only one participant outright denied support for political violence, stating that only "idiots would directly fight their own country." Possibly explaining his initial support on the survey, however, this participant appeared confused by the query as he initially answered as if we were asking about a war with China, in which case the participant said violence would indeed be necessary.

Two others appeared to show conflicting views on the subject. One participant began by offering a history lesson of the American Revolution and the justifications for that cause, but ultimately, the participant said, "As inefficient and frustrating as our government can be, I believe the overall process works. So, unless there is a supreme change to our rights and freedoms as we currently know them, it would have to be an extreme circumstance to be warranted to pick up arms against gov." Another veteran noted how 300 million people in the country have guns and was "surprised we haven't had more [political] violence" but then noted, "I don't think that violence is necessary or ever will be necessary."

Seven other participants appeared to speak directly of their support for political violence. Only two participants addressed this question in the first person. One participant stated, "There is a line in the sand that needs to be drawn," and also stated, "I have a line in the sand" and lamented that "Americans are way too fickle to rise up; It doesn't take a massive Army to overthrow the government. Most of these people are all talk and I'm not going to be the first one to step forward." Another respondent offered similar sentiments, stating that "I believe there is a major-league course correction that is needed" and also lamenting that "most will talk a hell of a game until it is time to do something and then they are not in the program anymore."

Others spoke more in the third person about the necessity of political violence, as if to distance themselves from the possible violence. One participant predicted martial law because the United States keeps "inching closer to" when "really horrible things will happen and people will have to defend themselves." Another observed that "there is going to be something that happens where people go, 'No.' . . . Something will stir something up so badly that people will have had enough." Another stated that "I am not inciting violence" but "if push comes to shove and they keep pushing," then "you" have to respond as if to a schoolyard bully.

Finally, a fourth participant noted that though it "sounds bad," violence "seems to be the only way to restore, to take back power to the people."

These participants offered a variety of rationales for what might warrant violence or tip the scales in its favor. One participant focused on the coronavirus disease 2019 (COVID-19) pandemic and highlighted the COVID-19 lockdowns, mask mandates, and vaccines, going so far as to note that although he would not kick down the door with his AR-15 if his child was vaccinated without his permission, "there is going to be a problem." Another participant listed overzealous government policies to curb climate change, restrictions on the Second Amendment, and the border crisis, which "is a powder keg for sure." Another spoke of First Amendment censorship; and a final participant declared, "You can vote your way into socialism, but you have to fight your way out."

Finally, one participant saw the 2024 presidential election as pivotal for the future of the country and is concerned that a Democratic win for the presidency, combined with further restrictions of the First and Second Amendments, would be grounds for civil war:

> I'll be the first to tell you [that] no way I want to see it happen, but I'll be the first to say it will go one of two ways. Depending on how [the] vote goes in 2024, if Democrats hold serve in '24, they will undo the First Amendment and the Second. Folks like me will say, "I can't win," we will become a totalitarian state, or they will say the Second Amendment was for one thing only, to go against the state. I can see a civil war; I hope it doesn't happen, but I can see it going that way. I talk to other people. They say we got the guns. Where are the military and police going to go. . . . If you listen to them talk about it and broach the subject, they are worried the left has enough firepower to [win the election], but I hope to God it doesn't happen. I just hope we do get a Republican president. I am very concerned. We are at the most critical point in terms of where this government goes. If the left wins, we will continue to see indoctrination we see in schools, the loss of the First Amendment, and we will lose the Second Amendment and the country will be gone with no place to go.

QAnon

We asked five participants about their professed views of the QAnon conspiracy theory, based on endorsement of QAnon on the 2022 survey.[1] We asked them specifically about the statement: "The government, media, and financial worlds in the U.S. are controlled by a group of Satan-worshipping pedophiles who run a global child sex-trafficking operation." Responses ranged from partial to full support for this conspiracy theory.

In response to this QAnon question, one participant stated, "That's crazy." However, when pressed further, the participant conceded belief in at least a part of the conspiracy theory by

[1] In two cases, participants had expressed support for QAnon in the survey, but, because of the length of the interviews, we were unable to ask them directly about their support.

stating that U.S. presidents do not make decisions to run the country and instead serve as puppets of "billionaires." Another participant initially laughed at the question and noted, "I didn't say that." But then the participant observed, "I don't think Epstein killed himself. . . . Who killed him and why? Maybe because he was flying rich pedophiles all over the world."

Three others were more direct in their support. One participant responded,

> That's 100 percent correct. I truly believe it. The Catholic Church is in on it. That's why they have orphanages all over the globe. It's all tied into the Epstein Island. People laugh about this because it's so sick and twisted, but I 100 percent agree with it. Where are all these missing kids going?

Another participant stated,

> I believe all of the [QAnon stuff] is true. . . . If you know anything about Hillary [Clinton] and her behavior and what she did to the children in Haiti, you would have a good understanding of what's going on. If you have seen anything off of Biden's computer, you would know. Where have all the children gone that were on the milk cartons when I was growing up?

A final participant, referring to "all the stuff with Hollywood and Epstein," said, it is "hard to believe something is not connected." He then referred to mysterious deaths that happen to people who put out information, and that conspiracy theorists are "right more often than wrong."

Great Replacement Theory

Fourteen participants in our study had affirmed support for the Great Replacement theory in the original 2022 survey—although, because of interview dynamics outside our control (including connection issues), we were only able to ask 11 of these individuals about their support during the 2023 interviews. Three of these 11 participants did not voice support for the Great Replacement theory during the 2023 interviews. For example, one participant stated, "No . . . I think you got to live and let live," "We focus on race and racial identity too much," and "I have not heard anything about that," in response to the survey item being spoken aloud.

However, eight of the 11 offered more clear-cut testimony of their belief in the conspiracy theory. In one case, the individual initially responded at first, "Not really, but the math does check out" before going on to express concern about the influx of immigrants coming into the country. In the remaining seven cases, participants directly stated that Democrats were allowing people to illegally cross the Southern U.S. border to amplify the Democratic vote. One participant stated, "Yeah the liberals are doing that, and that's why they have the open borders to get the democratic vote. Elections are rigged. . . . They are a bunch of lying cheats." Another said, "They are turning us into a third world country just because they think they will vote Democratic." And another responded, "Do I feel they are trying to replace native born? Yes, they are trying to flood the ballot box and become a one-party country. The Democrats are the ones who are doing it." Others variously stated, "Democrats are encouraging people coming in the country as they support their agenda," and that immigrants are being led through the Southern border "by Biden and his administration" and they are "probably going to vote for Biden." Another observed, "They are buying votes [through illegal immigration], and it really upsets me."

CHAPTER 3

Difficult Experiences in Military Service and the Transition to Civilian Life

In the following sections, we summarize participants' descriptions of difficult experiences during military service and while adapting to civilian life. We chose to summarize these experiences because so many of our respondents described such experiences;[1] 16 described difficult or traumatic experiences while serving; and 12 described struggles during the transition to civilian life.[2]

Experiences While Serving in the Military

Roughly three-quarters (15 out of 21) of our interviewees reported a disruptive or traumatic negative life event while in the military, ranging from interpersonal conflict (sometimes leading to discharge) to combat trauma to physical and sexual abuse. Several respondents described multiple challenging experiences and traumatic events during military service.

Six veterans (one female, right-leaning; five male, one left-leaning and four right-leaning) described disappointing or confusing interactions with commanding officers and the military bureaucracy, including confusion or coercion around being discharged, reenlisted, deployed, or redeployed to new locations.[3] For example:

> The war was brewing and I figured I was a Major halfway in and they weren't going to bother me. It was a shock to me when I got a letter. That was difficult because of the way we were brought on board. I had issues with the way the military didn't care—your number came up and you were going. After Desert Storm I stayed on and tried to resolve that issue too. Military people were brought on in the spur of the moment and let go in the spur of the moment. I didn't like it—if you were going to need me then you need to let me know. They called me up—I am not a piece of furniture—they called me up in February

[1] We do not assume any causal connection between these experiences and beliefs; see further discussion in Limitations.

[2] It is important to note that these patterns should be interpreted with reference to base rates of these experiences in the military, which is further discussed in our Limitations section.

[3] Such experiences are not necessarily unusual in the military. See Helmus et al., *Life as a Private*.

> and by late February I was there in [the facility]. . . . It was a real cluster—it wasn't done with a lot of preplanning. . . . This did screw up my relationship at home with my ex—she became my ex because she didn't like what was going on. It screwed up my relationship and I thought I had a pretty tight relationship.

Three male veterans (one left-leaning, two right-leaning) described combat trauma leading to posttraumatic stress disorder (PTSD) and another veteran struggles with mental health. One individual reported being a sniper during the Global War on Terror and noted that he had a formal PTSD diagnosis and experienced a "heightened sense of paranoia or anxiousness." Another talked about being in a helicopter crash during the Vietnam War that "messed me up, physically and more mentally," and how he, at least for some time, "did not feel safe and comfortable flying." Finally, another worked in the aftermath of the 1983 Beirut Barracks Bombing that killed 307 people including 220 Marines. This left-leaning veteran, who reports that he still suffers from PTSD, observed:

> When the Beirut bombing happened . . . we were involved in recovery identification and processes for young men who were killed. Whether you were civil engineering or supply it didn't matter. People stepped up and volunteered. That was a learning experience and [at the] same time one you won't forget because it shapes how you think about things in the future. So that had a profound effect on me, made me think of mortality in a different way because I was 20 years old, and the ones killed were 19–20 years old. And we lost friends on base due to accidents and after I left there was a bombing in the building I worked.

Three male veterans (two left-leaning, one right-leaning) described disciplinary issues while serving related to legal infractions and interpersonal conflict—in one case leading to imprisonment and in two cases leading to departure from service. For example, as one right-leaning veteran described:

> Unfortunately, I had an incident on the ship with a senior petty officer and he was kind of the poster board example of—I mean—I don't know that he ever was, but I wouldn't be surprised to find out that he was actually on a poster board for the U.S. Navy, and we both had a chip on our shoulders, and we got into a fight. Normally, it is quashed because there are so many of us, and I didn't think much about it. I was called in for a disciplinary review board and they reprimanded me and I was cut in rank. . . . and they confined me to the ship for 45 days. You can't leave the ship for 45 days and you are pier-side and all your friends are going out and you aren't and you aren't making too much money and now they've taken half of it. I wasn't allowed to bring any witnesses in and I decided in those 45 days that I'm out. It was too heavy handed for me.

Two male veterans (one left-leaning, one right-leaning) described struggling with excessive alcohol consumption while in the military, both to cope with the stresses of service and also to fit in socially. For example, one right-leaning participant described his heavy drinking in the service and noted that he hit a tree driving drunk at 80 mph soon after transitioning to civilian life. As he described it,

> Drinking was a big part of my life in the military—that was my crutch for the battles of everyday life—people telling you what to do and drill sergeants spitting in your face and just the routine. Once you sign on the dotted line, it was amazing how people talked to me different and treated me different. I was government property. I don't really like to take orders, so I was always in trouble—push-ups and stuff—but as far as the battle through everyday life, I just found drinking. The way people treat you in the military, everything is an order—they tell you when to go to bed, when to shower, when to exercise. Everything is told to you and demanded. I would just look forward to drinking every night, and that's how I battled through it, but it got me into a lot of trouble, too.

Finally, two female veterans (one left-leaning, one right-leaning) described severe physical, psychological, and sexual abuse at the hands of fellow service members. One left-leaning participant for example recalled multiple instances of sexual abuse and harassment. She noted that while attending to gunshot and blast wounds in a deployed medical facility, a senior officer sexually harassed her on a near "daily basis," and she was instructed by female noncommissioned officer not to "say anything." The experience left "a mark in terms of biochemicals and neurobiology" and a constant "state of alert." In another case, a right-leaning veteran recalled a commanding officer who "did not like White people" and "made it clear that women do not belong in the military." She said, "I was locked in a boiler room and he used to put me in a time-out and put me in a boiler room and told me I could not stand up and leave me in there for hours." Observing its impact, the veteran noted, "It was a long time ago now and I'm over it, but I was pretty upset."

Struggles During Transition to Civilian Life

Twelve participants described difficulties with the transition from military to civilian life, including feeling lonely and longing for the pace and camaraderie of military life, having no transition resources and not knowing where to turn, and economic and legal struggles—even becoming homeless and ending up in prison. As with negative experiences during military service, several veterans described multiple transition-related struggles.

Eight veterans (four male right-leaning, two male left-leaning, one female right-leaning, one female left-leaning) described suffering from emotional and behavioral issues while adapting to civilian life, including residual anger or being "wound up" from military service, dealing with PTSD and depression, and ongoing substance use issues. For example, one left-leaning male veteran described,

> I was wound up, I was not in kill mode, I was in p----d mode, as I was not kicked out fairly. I was given a negative discharge and I was not educated on the facts of my discharge. And my girl was still overseas, and that kind of hurt. I was just in p----d mode, like f--- it all.

> But I see other people that go through those different modes and transitions and they become alcoholics and drugs addicts and wind up dead.

These emotional and behavioral struggles resulted in arrest or imprisonment for two male veterans (one left-leaning, one right-leaning). As one right-leaning veteran noted,

> I have a few small criminal issues. . . . The times I have had warrants served it was ten or twelve cops. One was a reckless driving charge doing drag racing after I came back from Iraq. [My wife] woke me up and told me there was someone in the bushes in our yard in the middle of the day. There were a lot of squad cars there and they came to arrest me for reckless endangerment. I heard from one of the arresting officers that someone had told them I just got back from Iraq, so I guess they felt they had to ensure I wasn't crazy.

In several cases, veterans linked these emotional and behavioral struggles with challenges in their marriages or romantic relationships.

Six veterans (two female, one left-leaning and one right-leaning; four male, one left-leaning and three right-leaning) described missing the camaraderie and pace of the military. These experiences were often temporary, lasting only months or a few years. For example, one male right-leaning veteran described, "When I was trying to adapt to civilian life, because in the military, we were told when to eat, when to go to bed, and I was now waiting around for someone to tell me what to do and where to go. And in the first few months, it was hard." In other cases, veterans described these experiences as severe and long-lasting. For example, a politically conservative veteran observed,

> I went into a depression that I was not expecting. . . . Staying at home after feeling important and being around so many people—even though the camaraderie wasn't always what it should have been—you are part of something so big. Then going to being home with a newborn was very isolated. I felt like I didn't have a purpose, and I have heard it is very common. . . . I think there is always going to be a loneliness inside me, because for years you never have a moment to yourself. You are part of something so big. . . . I feel like there is always going to be this little void—like, this loneliness.

Meanwhile, six male veterans (four right-leaning, two left-leaning) described having difficulties getting on their feet economically, struggles often described as temporary and only lasting a few months or years. For example, one right-leaning male veteran described,

> I graduated college in 2009, when I was getting out of the [military branch of service]. I had it in my mind that I was going to be a professional businessman. This was not the best time for college graduates entering [the workforce and looking for] employment and housing after leaving the military. . . . I had all those dreams of starting off in a business environment, but there were none of those to make money in.

In two cases (one right-leaning, one left-leaning), male veterans faced such severe economic challenges, including facing housing issues. For example:

> After I left the military, I went right to my parents' house, and instantly . . . when you get out, the problem is, you don't have anything. If you didn't save any money—I didn't save any money because you don't make much money. I made, what was it, I think $300 a week, but I didn't have to pay for housing and food, which helped, but you are only making $1,200 a month. It's not like you're going to come home with like $10–20K in your pocket and just buy a vehicle and go to work. It doesn't work like that. I had to go to my parents and slowly do side jobs and take buses and stuff just to get a vehicle so I could get a job and then move on with my life. So you're pretty much on your own. And if you are a weak or a lazy person, you are going to wind up on unemployment and on the streets very quickly.

Finally, four veterans (three males, two left-leaning and one right-leaning; one left-leaning female) described having little to no support from the military or U.S. Department of Veterans Affairs (VA) when trying to make the transition to civilian life. As one liberal veteran observed,

> And then when I got out, I felt used. Now what? What do I do? There was zero authentic support. They throw you brochures, do this. But none of it is authentic or culturally relevant, and none of it prepares you for the crash that you have. Because from a neurology standpoint, all those hormones raging in your system have gone to zero and you have to figure out that gap for a normal existence in the civilian world. It was very lonely, very hard, there is not a ton that was done that was authentic or helpful.

The Path to Current Beliefs

As part of our interviews, we asked participants what helped shape their current political beliefs and whether they discussed politics or related beliefs with anyone (whether like-minded or not). Finally, we asked about media sources that they used to "stay informed" on political issues. The following sections describe these results; specifically, respondents talked about their political beliefs being shaped by major events in history and their personal experiences of those events (12 cases). They also talked about their social environment helping to shape and reinforce their political beliefs (12 cases), and consuming various forms of media and social media (16 cases). In these discussions, participants drew a more direct line between these experiences and their beliefs and/or support for different extremist groups.

Political Events and Turning Points

When talking about their political viewpoints and current activism, 12 participants noted one or more specific experiences in life or moments in time when they started to become more politically involved. These included experiences connected with military service or in work settings, notable events in national politics, and life disruptions during COVID-19.

Six male veterans (two left-leaning, four right-leaning) focused on global and national politics and noted events such as different presidential administrations, the rise of Trump and January 6, or the attack on 9/11 as inspiration to start paying more attention to politics and becoming more involved in political causes. For example, one right-leaning participant stated that he started "paying attention" when he saw President Barack Obama say the United States is not a Christian nation. He noted, "we are a Judeo-Christian nation . . . ," our country is "literally founded on Levitical laws." Another right-leaning participant dated it back to the U.S. Supreme Court case of Bush v. Gore that decided the 2000 presidential election. "That was eye-opening for me. Been into politics ever since." Another case looked back to the President Ronald Reagan years. As he observed,

> I was well into Reagan when he was in. I saw what was going on. Back in the '70s, I was for the Democrats, and then Reagan comes in and he was Democratic and then turned Republican and I was in the military. I was like whoa, the Republicans were the Democrats, and the Democrats were the Republicans of today. So, I got heavy into Reaganomics. I realized that the smaller the government the more focused they were on the people's needs, not the oligarchs. . . . Now, after Trump, I hear all this stuff about Trump, and I had to research it for myself and saw what the Democrats were doing and thought this is wrong. So, I changed to Republican because I saw the needs of the people being met under Trump.

Four veterans described having specific experiences during or directly after military service or while in law enforcement careers that changed or strengthened their political views. These included exposure to foreign countries and comparison with conditions in the United States. Two right-leaning male veterans described returning home from Vietnam as inspiration for switching from radical left-wing beliefs to becoming more right-leaning. For example:

> I survived [Vietnam] of course and came home and the world was upside down. Spiro Agnew was chased out, after Nixon, gas prices were high and everything doubled in price, gas from 20 cents to a dollar a gallon. And they brought me back to [military base] and [the] gas shortage was real. I was in culture shock; it was not the country I left. And my political views changed. I was not the [left-wing] radical I was once, especially after having been overseas and seeing how world operates. . . . It was so unfair too; we were not allowed to win in Vietnam. They were too afraid of China getting involved and no way they were going to turn it loose and get it done. . . . I was grateful for my experience and changed my viewpoint of myself and the world and gave me appreciation of what it was about. I came out and I was 24 and had more direction which the military provided me . . . . I voted for Ronald Reagan and my views began to change a lot more.

Meanwhile, two veterans (one male right-leaning, one female right-leaning) also described being exposed to chaos and upheaval in the United States while serving in law enforcement as political turning points for their own beliefs. For example, one female right-leaning veteran described how this occurred while acting as a first responder during the Black Lives Matter riots after the 2020 death of George Floyd sparked protests:

> In the summer of 2020, [rioters] burned down my city, they burned down squad cars. I got shot at twice. A firetruck had to come. They started pulling the firemen out of the truck. I did not think I was going to live. I stepped on a used condom. There was an 8–9 month lady pregnant. . . . I'm so confident that I'm correct in my beliefs. When that pregnant lady showed me her a--hole, I could see that was the devil. I was already strong, but I kept telling my partner, "You see?" When you see a heroin overdose and the guy has his eyes rolled back? That is demonic possession.

Finally, three right-leaning male veterans described COVID-19 and the subsequent lockdowns, as well as the effects that these lockdowns had on their personal lives and economic well-being, as inspirations for becoming involved politically. For example:

> [T]here is a line in the sand that needs to be drawn. . . . We got shut down on St. Patrick's Day, we got shut down like everyone else. We are closing at 5 o'clock, they said—everyone is. That was it—that was my wife's primary job, and we were out of work, and the way COVID went, we got our jobs back after a while and we got our jobs back. But the mayor decided it wasn't safe enough to have New Year's celebrations, but there was nothing she could do—excuse me, this is a tourist destination! So she put in a lockdown for pretty much a four-day weekend. New Year's Eve was on a Thursday, and for the entirety of the weekend she put in a curfew. . . . our family had already lost the money. I didn't resort to violence, but I have a line drawn in the sand. At some point, to enforce these things—it said you couldn't go outside of your house after 10 p.m. We had cops that put hands on people because they weren't putting masks on by themselves.

Socialization Through Family and Peers

Thirteen of our interviewees also explained how they were socialized into their current viewpoints through friends or family, and how their social circles provide support and encouragement for their beliefs.

Six veterans (three left-leaning and three right-leaning participants) described how they share political viewpoints with their family members, and some even described being influenced by their parents and in turn influencing their own children in a political way. For example, one right-leaning veteran explained, "My daddy had those views, too. I was kind of brought up with that kind of stuff. My daughter is 100 percent on board, and my son is about 50 percent or maybe 70 percent on board." A different right-leaning veteran explained how, "I have a network of people, my cousin and my brother, because we are serious about this. We do this back and forth, like a pooling of information." One left-leaning veteran described how early family influence factored into his political views: "My family leans toward my perspective, my parents are very well read, they didn't go to college, but they prized the ability to do research and it is something they taught us growing up so [you've] got to constantly look for [the] source, find the facts, don't react to what people tell you."

Four veterans, three of whom were right-leaning, talked about sports or other clubs with participants with very similar viewpoints. For example, one veteran explained, "The most political talk that goes on is my sportsman club. Obviously, I don't hunt anymore but I do shoot a pistol and we are interested in gun laws and the Second Amendment. We have one guy who is retired [officer rank] from [military branch of service] and he . . . is following this stuff and he reports at our monthly meeting on legislation that is going on." Another veteran described having a large network of like-minded activists with whom he met regularly either face-to-face or electronically:

> I have 100 friends that I can trust and have the key to my place. I have 100 percent respect for them, and they have respect for me. I am not fighting this battle alone—I have several people who are right on board with me. We meet three times a week to put documents together and fight the battle. . . . There's a lot of people that are digging. One person is really into child trafficking, another person is really into probate court and that information goes around the group. Videos, writings, people doing their own writing and documents, and then that group expands. We have 250 people who are part of the group, but they have friends and relatives and cousins that expand it out too.

Three right-leaning veterans described sharing and mutually reinforcing political viewpoints with other military and/or law enforcement colleagues in work settings. For example, one veteran explained, "Most of my friends and acquaintances are former law enforcement. We do deal with, there are some civilians we associate with but mostly law enforcement. I've run across a liberal in law enforcement, but that is 1 percent. If you want to reinforce your thinking, hang out with law enforcement." Another veteran described first developing her political thinking while in the military:

> When I got into the military, I started to get into conspiracy theories because of conversations with my peers. That's when I learned about the Illuminati—the elites like Lady Gaga, Elon Musk—a bunch of satanists that run the world. Then that explains so much and from there just a rabbit hole of things unraveling. All the corruption about the government. I never thought when I enlisted that I would [be] fighting wars. . . . I always trusted them. I had heard things about 9/11 and stuff but I always trusted. Seeing all of the stupid things—like we guard our nuclear weapons with Master Locks and I became very mistrustful. Now I'm a full tin hat.

Meanwhile, one left-leaning veteran described building and accentuating his left-leaning views while working for local government and nonprofit organizations. Additionally, another veteran described meeting other disaffected veterans in college and starting to mobilize with that group into left wing politics.

Three left-leaning veterans described becoming politically aware in high school or college settings. One left-leaning male veteran described this as an "intellectual bug":

> I've been politically engaged since high school. I worked the polls once I got 18 before going into the military. I felt I needed the knowledge to do that job, so history and political science have been a fascination for years. I studied the politics of war. I looked at that from the Middle Ages and no difference from then to now.

Meanwhile, another veteran explained:

> I was at city college and saw sign for where vets were going to be speaking, so I checked it out and it was this org that was not your usual patriotism, nationalism, fascist organization of white bros that everyone loves to trot out. They started criticizing imperialism. They were talking about their own experiences in Afghanistan and Iraq and I realized there were a lot of the same themes from my experience and that led me to connect the dots and think about, are we the baddies? Yes, we are the baddies. In my mind the military is just poor American people sent off to be hired guns to kill other poor people around the world for profit.

Media and Social Media

Roughly three-quarters (16 out of 21) of respondents mentioned specific media sources, social media platforms, and podcasters or political influencers that currently helped shape their viewpoints and kept them up to date. These ranged from CNN and Fox News to Russia Today and Newsmax, from Facebook to specific Reddit or Telegram channels, and from podcaster Joe Rogan to television host George Stephanopoulos. One left-leaning veteran described being kicked off of Facebook/Meta repeatedly for misinformation and hate speech, and even discussing this issue during counseling sessions. A right-leaning veteran described using Facebook comments to try to influence others' beliefs:

> People say you are arguing with [name of friend] on Facebook and you won't convince him. I realize that I won't be able to do this, but I want someone else who is reading it to maybe change their mind, or I can arm them with—when someone says this online— you can say this in return. . . . I graduated [high school] in 2003, and that was the advent of social media, and obviously it's gotten stronger. I wasn't always arguing abortion. You can pick a topic, or you can let society pick the topic for you. You can find something you disagree with and just hit them [with a comment].

Another right-leaning veteran described mostly staying off of social media but consuming specific books and videos; "I learned about the banking system because [of the] *All Wars Are Bankers' Wars* video. *The Creature of Jekyll Island* by Edward Griffin is a book. It's about Klaus Schwab and the World Economic Forum and what they are trying to do and all of the other organizations that have been put together to try to bring down this system." Meanwhile, one left-leaning veteran described staying active across a wide variety of platforms, including those on the right-leaning wing:

> Democracy Now, Aljazeera, RT, so many. Also, by virtue of being an educated and aware person I have to keep tabs on all of it. I keep tabs on CNN, MSNBC, Fox, Breitbart when they were around. I tried to have as much a varied if you will from all of the sides, bottom, left, right. I don't think it is healthy to zone in on one. It is not healthy for a thinking person. . . . Social media? 100 percent. It's even more important now. Because of all the moves that Elon Musk is making he is now blowing up his own site, which used to be very reliable for breaking news. I don't know many in my generation who are watching the news. So, Twitter was the fastest one and it would be there in the morning and, two to three days later, show up on Instagram or Facebook, but now it is getting more difficult because of all the mess that Mr. Musk is doing. Yeah, it is important to have a diversity of channels and sources.

No veterans with whom we spoke talked about creating content (other than comments on posts) on social media; the one veteran (male and right-leaning) who spent a lot of time creating content distributed this via email to a group of roughly 250.

CHAPTER 4

Limitations and Discussion

Limitations

First, we should note that this study has several limitations. Because this is a small qualitative study that only focused on those participants who had expressed some support for an extremist belief or group on our previous survey, it is difficult to make inferences about causal pathways to extremism. We interviewed 21 veterans out of 32 with whom we had appointments, themselves a subsample of 84 who agreed to be contacted, and 137 out of approximately 1,000 veterans in total who expressed such a belief or support for a group. Thus, although our survey sample was nationally representative, our qualitative sample represents 15 percent of our eligible population, and it is difficult to know how biased (and in what ways) our final qualitative sample was (see Table 1 for qualitative sample characteristics versus the total eligible population).

Additionally, we only conducted interviews with "cases"; that is, we did not interview veterans from our survey who did not express support for any extremist beliefs or groups. Thus, we cannot assess the degree to which military experiences, the transition to civilian life, social experiences, and the like in our sample are different or unique from other veterans. Similarly, although we were struck by both the proportion of our sample that described difficult or traumatic experiences during and after military service, any comparison of this with nationally representative statistics would be fraught, given the size of our sample.

Although our overall approach to the study (first conducting a survey and then following up with a subsample) is sound, we made a few compromises in our recruitment and interviewing strategy. For example, anticipating issues with trust and rapport, we did not present participants with their survey responses directly or challenge them if their interview responses differed from survey responses. Also, to establish rapport and ease into the discussion regarding political beliefs, we did not try to establish links between military and other life experiences and current political beliefs. This prevented us from developing a detailed timeline of political beliefs that could provide more direct inferences regarding the sequence of life events and political beliefs and actions.

Finally, one of our survey findings was that members of the Marine Corps showed more pronounced endorsement of extremist groups, and we simply did not have the sample (only a single Marine Corps veteran) to explore any service branch–specific pathways or characteristics. This finding might reflect bias in our recruiting and eventual sample, something that a larger sample or a focused service branch quota approach to recruiting could solve.

Discussion

As far as we know, this is the first study to use systematic qualitative methods to examine the potential pathways to extremism among veterans. Therefore, this field of research is in its infancy, and our own study has many methodological limitations that should caution its use for specific policy recommendations.

The main take-home lesson of our study is the tremendous heterogeneity underlying what seems like cut-and-dried survey data. Specifically, when asked about political beliefs and support for groups, respondents provided many different rationales, ranging from wholesale retractions (or corrections, perhaps) of survey responses, to qualifications and careful rationales, to full-throated endorsement with statements of readiness for action. Four who stated in the 2022 survey that they supported the Proud Boys now retracted that support, although it is unclear whether such retractions were due to a change of heart or recognition that affirming such support was not socially acceptable (if the latter, this could indicate that surveys might provide better assessments of support for publicly unpopular groups or beliefs). Support for QAnon varied from those seeing a secret cabal running the government to others outright concerned that this cabal consisted of pedophiles stealing and sexually abusing children. The most homogenous views were held by those supporting the Great Replacement theory, with the vast majority certain that the Democratic Party was allowing illegal immigration as a way to "buy" votes.

Participant responses to questions about political violence provide an instructive example. Scholars have expressed alarm about the high levels of support for political violence found in other surveys. For example, surveys suggest that 19 percent of the public supports political violence, and our previous survey of veterans in 2022 suggested that nearly 18 percent offered such support.[1] These findings have led to fears that that the United States is on the cusp of a civil war.[2] What do our interviews say about this? First, some participants, while conflicted about the political situation, seem to deny outright support for violence. Others affirmed their support for this question, but few, if any, seemed poised for action. These individuals spoke passively about the need for violence and stated, "People . . . will have to defend themselves" or "will have had enough," or that violence "seems to be the only way to restore the country." Two seemed more serious on this issue and spoke in the first person about drawing a "line in the sand" or believing a "course correction was needed." Two others lamented

1 Helmus, Brown, and Ramchand, *Prevalence of Veteran Support for Extremist Groups and Extremist Beliefs*.

2 Walter, "These Are Conditions Ripe for Political Violence."

how few are willing to act and stated that they would not be the first ones to do so. Hence, although the number of participants who were willing to use the language of violence to discuss political change may be a harbinger of future strife, none was poised to act on violence in the near term. These complexities regarding support for political violence provide a caution to any straightforward interpretation of survey data on extremist beliefs and support for extremist groups, whether with veterans or other groups.[3]

Given prior research on the development of support for extremism,[4] we were somewhat surprised not to hear more about support for specific groups and the ideological rationale for supporting such groups. This finding might be in part because the set of beliefs underlying support for these groups is much more widespread (and perhaps also socially acceptable) than explicit support for such groups themselves. Also, based on prior work,[5] we were surprised at the relative lack of discussion regarding bottom-up recruitment to current beliefs via peer groups; however, such reporting might also have been affected by an abundance of caution on the part of respondents.

A second major observation is the degree to which participants described having difficult and even traumatic experiences during their military service and during their transition to civilian life. Three quarters of the participants made a point to describe major negative events that occurred during military service, and these ranged from conflict with senior officers to traumatic experiences of combat and even physical and sexual abuse. Prior work has shown that the bureaucratic and interpersonal hassles of military life loom large in narratives of military service members. In a previous RAND study in which researchers conducted in-depth interviews with more than 80 U.S. Army privates, soldiers reported a variety of hassles from long work hours to strife with leadership and fellow soldiers to excessive downtime.[6] Still, many of these issues were considered minor and most spoke in positive terms about their satisfaction with Army and unit life. Although our sample had some positive things to say about military life, most focused on one or more negative or traumatic events while in the military. It is noteworthy that analyses by the University of Maryland's START found that, of those with U.S. military backgrounds who committed mass casualty attacks, 32.1 percent had failed to receive an honorable discharge from the military.[7] In addition, although some scholars talk about the connection between posttraumatic stress and combat experi-

[3] Other studies that have attempted alternate formulations of the political violence question have indicated that the assumptions underlying our survey items may not be sound, and that such questions may thus overestimate the propensity or readiness for political violence (see Westwood et al., "Current Research Overstates American Support for Political Violence").

[4] For example, see Davis and Cragin, *Social Science for Counterterrorism*.

[5] For example, see Zech and Gabbay, "Social Network Analysis in the Study of Terrorism and Insurgency."

[6] Helmus et al., *Life as a Private*.

[7] Jensen, Kane, and Akers, *Mass Casualty Extremist Offenders with U.S. Military Backgrounds*.

ence and radicalization,[8] establishing a causal link between personal trauma and radicalization remains difficult due to both the small number of known cases and the degree to which trauma's role appears to be contingent on many other personal and social circumstances.[9]

More than one-half of our participants reported problems while transitioning out of military service and into civilian life. These participants described periods of loneliness after a military life often marked by close bonds among fellow service personnel, as well as economic struggles. These experiences are echoed in the broader academic literature. Recent RAND research on the economic experience of transition suggests that many veterans do initially earn less money when first moving to civilian life.[10] Other reports also attest to the interpersonal and social struggles that attend separation from the service.[11] Previous work has highlighted how military transition issues may pose a risk factor for political extremism.[12] Extremist groups, for all their malign impacts on society, do provide individuals with a sense of social support and belonging—hence, the reasoning goes, lonely veterans may be at risk.[13]

However, it is difficult to make an explicit causal connection between military or transition experiences in our study. First, very few of our participants directly connected their negative military or transition experiences to their political beliefs or to the evolution of such beliefs. Second, it is unclear whether the military or transition experiences they described were unusual for veterans in terms of severity or duration. Finally, when participants did describe the factors that led to their beliefs, such discussions focused more on political events than hardships experienced during the transition to military life. It is not uncommon for individuals thick in the thrall of group-driven coping mechanisms (including extremist groups) to be unable to recognize the role of their own trauma or life struggles in driving their beliefs or group membership; such realization is often guided by experts during therapeutic processes associated with deradicalization.[14]

We believe future research should attempt to tease out the relative importance of negative experiences in the military, transition stress, and other potential risk factors on the path to radicalization for veterans. These factors are especially important given the earlier referenced findings from START of veteran involvement in mass casualty attacks.[15] Our 2022 survey

8 Speckhard, Ellenberg, and Garret, "The Challenge of Extremism in the Military Is Not Going Away Without a New Perspective."

9 For example, see Jensen, Atwell Seate, and James, "Radicalization to Violence."

10 Goldman et al., *Navigating a Big Transition.*

11 Wilson, Hill, and Kiernan, "Loneliness and Social Isolation of Military Veterans"; Graham, "Combating Social Isolation and Loneliness Among Veterans After Separation from Military Service."

12 Helmus, Brown, and Ramchand, "How to Put RAND Findings on Veteran Support for Extremism in Context."

13 Brown et al., *Violent Extremism in America.*

14 For example, see Aarten, Mulder, and Pemberton, "The Narrative of Victimization and Deradicalization."

15 Jensen, Kane, and Akers, *Mass Casualty Extremist Offenders with U.S. Military Backgrounds.*

examining veteran support for extremist groups and causes was limited in that we were only able to allocate a limited number of questions to the overall survey instrument—hence, we could not ask respondents about such military experiences as combat, PTSD, or challenges associated with transition to veteran status. Given that respondents in our study identified issues with their experiences in and transiting out of military service, it seems that a more robust survey that can systematically examine such experiences and correlate them with extremist beliefs may be warranted. It would be even better if such a future survey enlisted both representative samples of veterans and nonveterans alike and calibrated the relative risk of veteran extremism across demographic categories.[16] Additionally, we believe that follow-up qualitative and quantitative research with a larger sample of both cases and *non-cases* (e.g., those attesting to and those denying extremist views) will be important to sort out causal pathways for veterans that become radicalized.

This study did not specifically examine policies that could help limit risks of veteran extremism. We will note however that such policies must be carefully calibrated so as not to risk disenfranchising veterans from utilizing the services of the VA agency or seeking care at VA hospitals. For example, a campaign that sought to counter the ideological roots of veteran extremism could quickly backfire.[17] However, the VA undertakes the critical mission of supporting military personnel transition to civilian life, offering support for veteran economic, social, and emotional needs.[18] These efforts have enormous value for the general well-being of veterans. If future research confirms the potential role of transition in veteran radicalization, then such programs could also play a critical role in terrorism prevention.

[16] Helmus, Brown, and Ramchand, "How to Put RAND Findings on Veteran Support for Extremism in Context."

[17] Walsh, "Policymakers Say Addressing Extremism Among Veterans Is a 'Delicate' Challenge."

[18] U.S. Department of Veterans Affairs, "Outreach, Transition and Economic Development: Your VA Transition Assistance Program (TAP)."

APPENDIX A

Interview Instrument

Interview Instrument In-Depth Conversations with Veterans

Based on your responses to our survey, we expect you may be able to help us understand more about current social dynamics in the U.S. and related topics like U.S. politics and polarization, and/or why people are joining different groups or movements.

We are particularly interested in the experiences and opinions of veterans about this issue, which is why we have followed up with you.

Please remember, if you tell me that you intend to hurt yourself or someone else, I will report it to my supervisor, who may report it to the authorities.

1. **Please tell me a bit about your military service?**
   a. What branch of service were you in and what role or Military Occupational Specialty (MOS)?
   b. What were your experiences like when you were serving?
   c. How well supported did you feel when you were in the service?

2. **What was it like for you when you transitioned out of the military?**
   a. How well supported did you feel in your transition to veteran status?

3. **What is your life like right now? Please tell me how things are going for you and what's most important in your life at the moment?**
   a. What are you doing for work now [but please do not name your employer or offer any identifying information]?
   b. What are your relationships like with family and friends?

4. **In our survey, we asked about your support for different political movements and organizations. Could I identify a few of these movements and ask what you think?**
   a. First, what about Democratic or Republican political party? Are you into politics at all?
   b. What about Proud Boys. What are your thoughts about that movement?

   c. Another organization is Antifa (follow with Black nationalism, White supremacists as necessary).

5. **Thank you for sharing this. Could you tell us a bit more about [name of org/belief that respondent affirmed in original survey]?**
   a. In what ways do you find this {movement/group} appealing?
   b. Some people who have these beliefs feel isolated, others have folks they can talk to? What about you, are there others who share these beliefs that you interact with? (Are any of them veterans)?
   c. What kinds of experiences led you to support this {movement/group}?
   d. What are the best things about {movement/group}?
   e. And what are the worst?

Q&A Guidance

A. **Why did you choose me?** We did a survey that asked about political movements and beliefs and you had indicated some support for such movements
B. **Do you have my survey results there?** I do, but we want to get beyond these survey results and talk about what you believe now and we want to have a more extended conversation about these beliefs.
C. **Was your publication the same survey I did?** Yes, that survey helped us with our publication
D. **Do you believe in any of these?** I found some of these items challenging but I have been instructed not to talk my views. I really want to know what you think.

Abbreviations

9/11	September 11, 2001, terrorist attacks
COVID-19	coronavirus disease 2019
KKK	Ku Klux Klan
NORC	National Opinion Research Center
PTSD	posttraumatic stress disorder
START	National Consortium for the Study of Terrorism and Responses to Terrorism
VA	U.S. Department of Veterans Affairs

References

Aarten, Pauline G. M., Eva Mulder, and Antony Pemberton, "The Narrative of Victimization and Deradicalization: An Expert View," *Studies in Conflict & Terrorism*, Vol. 41, No. 7, 2018.

Anti-Defamation League, "QAnon," backgrounder, September 24, 2020. As of April 21, 2023: https://www.adl.org/resources/backgrounder/qanon

Brown, Ryan Andrew, Todd C. Helmus, Rajeev Ramchand, Alina I. Palimaru, Sarah Weilant, Ashley L. Rhoades, and Liisa Hiatt, *Violent Extremism in America: Interviews with Former Extremists and Their Families on Radicalization and Deradicalization*, RAND Corporation, RR-A1071-1, 2021. As of December 29, 2023: https://www.rand.org/pubs/research_reports/RRA1071-1.html

Davis, Paul K. and Kim Cragin, eds., *Social Science for Counterterrorism: Putting the Pieces Together*, RAND Corporation, MG-849-OSD, 2009. As of February 15, 2024: https://www.rand.org/pubs/monographs/MG849.html

George Washington University Program on Extremism, "Capitol Hill Siege: Demographics Tracker," webpage, undated. As of February 27, 2024: https://extremism.gwu.edu/Capitol-Hill-Siege

Goldman, Charles A., Jeremy Boback, Robert Bozick, and Drew M. Anderson, *Navigating a Big Transition: Military Service Members' Earnings and Employment After Active-Duty Service*, RAND Corporation, RR-A361-1, 2021. As of December 20, 2023: https://www.rand.org/pubs/research_reports/RRA361-1.html

Graham, Emily, "Combating Social Isolation and Loneliness Among Veterans After Separation from Military Service," Syracuse University, Issue Brief No. 59, December 6, 2022.

Helmus, Todd C., Ryan Andrew Brown, and Rajeev Ramchand, "How to Put RAND Findings on Veteran Support for Extremism in Context," *RAND Blog*, September 11, 2023a. As of December 28, 2023: https://www.rand.org/pubs/commentary/2023/09/how-to-put-rand-findings-on-veteran-support-for-extremism.html

Helmus, Todd C., Ryan Andrew Brown, and Rajeev Ramchand, *Prevalence of Veteran Support for Extremist Groups and Extremist Beliefs: Results from a Nationally Representative Survey of the U.S. Veteran Community*, RAND Corporation, RR-A1071-2-v2, 2023b. As of December 28, 2023: https://www.rand.org/pubs/research_reports/RRA1071-2-v2.html

Helmus, Todd C., S. Rebecca Zimmerman, Marek N. Posard, Jasmine L. Wheeler, Cordaye Ogletree, Quinton Stroud, and Margaret C. Harrell, *Life as a Private: A Study of the Motivations and Experiences of Junior Enlisted Personnel in the U.S. Army*, RAND Corporation, RR-2252-A, 2018. As of December 29, 2023: https://www.rand.org/pubs/research_reports/RR2252.html

Jensen, Michael A., Sheehan Kane, and Elena Akers, "Extremism in the Ranks and After," National Consortium for the Study of Terrorism and Responses to Terrorism, webpage, August 2023a. As of December 29, 2023: https://www.start.umd.edu/publication/extremism-ranks-and-after

Jensen, Michael A., Sheehan Kane, and Elena Akers, *Mass Casualty Extremist Offenders with U.S. Military Backgrounds*, National Consortium for the Study of Terrorism and Responses to Terrorism, June 2023b.

Jensen, Michael A., Anita Atwell Seate, and Patrick A. James, "Radicalization to Violence: A Pathway Approach to Studying Extremism," *Terrorism and Political Violence*, Vol. 32, No. 5, 2020.

Jensen, Michael A., Elizabeth Yates, and Sheehan Kane, *Radicalization in the Ranks: An Assessment of the Scope and Nature of Criminal Extremism in the United States Military*, National Consortium for the Study of Terrorism and Responses to Terrorism, January 2022.

Jones, Seth G., Catrina Doxsee, and Nicholas Harrington, *The Escalating Terrorism Problem in the United States*, Center for Strategic and International Studies, June 2020.

Jones, Seth G., "Violent Domestic Extremist Groups and the Recruitment of Veterans," Center for Strategic & International Studies, October 13, 2021.

Kutner, Samantha, *Swiping Right: The Allure of Hyper Masculinity and Cryptofascism for Men Who Join the Proud Boys*, International Centre for Counter-Terrorism, May 2020.

Levine, Peter K., Joseph F. Adams, Amy A. Alrich, Rachel G. Augustine, Margaret D. M. Barber, Sujeeta B. Bhatt, Kathleen M. Conley, et al., *Prohibited Extremist Activities in the U.S. Department of Defense*, Institute for Defense Analysis, No. P-33076, December 2023.

Rothbart, Daniel, and David M. Stebbins, "The Proud Boys Raging Righteously at the US Capitol on January 6, 2021: A Hate Group in Action," *Peace and Conflict: Journal of Peace Psychology*, Vol. 29, No. 4, 2023.

Speckhard, Anne, and Molly Ellenberg, *An Analysis of Active-Duty and Veteran Military Members Involved in White Supremacist and Violent Anti-Government Militias and Groups: 2017–2022*, International Center for the Study of Violent Extremism, 2023.

Speckhard, Anne, Molly Ellenberg, and T. M. Garret, "The Challenge of Extremism in the Military Is Not Going Away Without a New Perspective," *Military Times*, November 16, 2021.

Toropin, Konstantin, and Steve Beynon, "Veterans Make Up Most of Proud Boys Members Indicted on Sedition for Jan 6 Violence," *Military.com*, June 7, 2022.

U.S. Census Bureau, "Veterans Day 2023: November 11," press release, October 19, 2023. As of January 5, 2024:
https://www.census.gov/newsroom/facts-for-features/2023/veterans-day.html.

U.S. Department of Veterans Affairs, "Outreach, Transition and Economic Development: Your VA Transition Assistance Program (TAP)," webpage, undated. As of January 10, 2024:
https://www.benefits.va.gov/transition/tap.asp

Walsh, Steve, "Policymakers Say Addressing Extremism Among Veterans Is a 'Delicate' Challenge," American Homefront, December 30, 2022.

Walter, Barbara F., "These Are Conditions Ripe for Political Violence: How Close Is the US to Civil War," *The Guardian*, November 6, 2022.

Westwood, Sean J., Justin Grimmer, Matthew Tyler, and Clayton Nall, "Current Research Overstates American Support for Political Violence," *Proceedings of the National Academy of Sciences*, Vol. 119, No. 12, 2022.

Wilson, G., M. Hill and M. D. Kiernan, "Loneliness and Social Isolation of Military Veterans: Systematic Narrative Review," *Occupational Medicine*, Vol. 68, No. 9, December 2018.

Zech, Steven T., and Michael Gabbay, "Social Network Analysis in the Study of Terrorism and Insurgency: From Organization to Politics," *International Studies Review*, Vol. 18, No. 2, 2016.